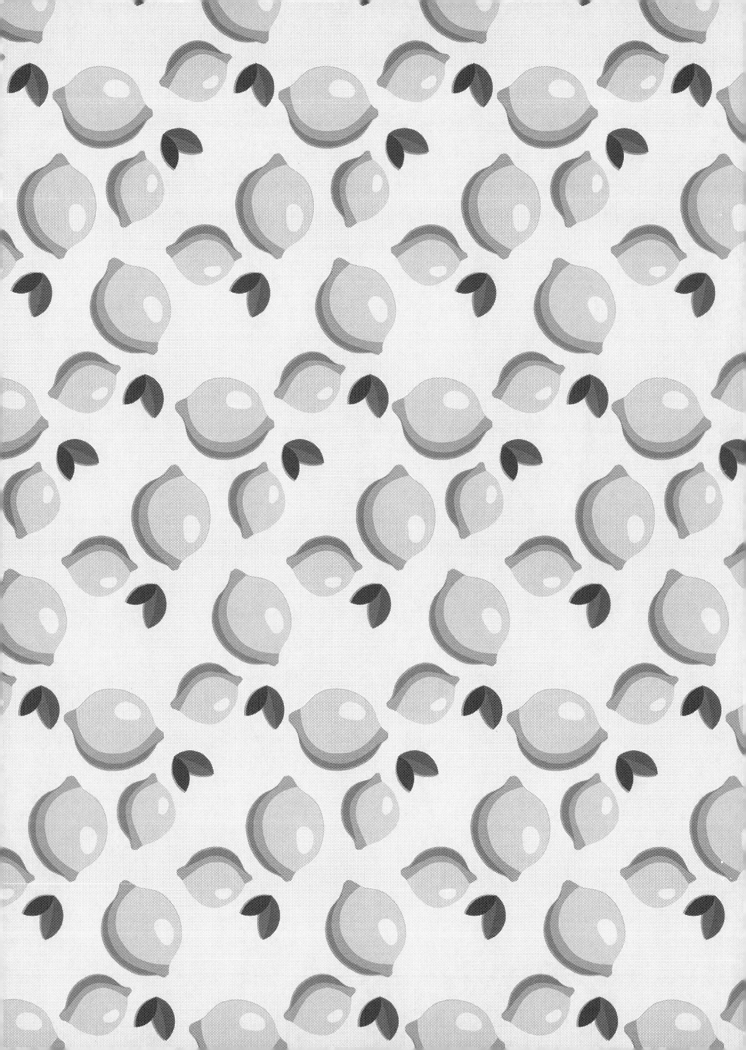

How to Make
Lemonade

A Christian's Guide to Success

Lady Terran Jordan

authorHOUSE®

AuthorHouse™
1663 Liberty Drive
Bloomington, IN 47403
www.authorhouse.com
Phone: 1 (800) 839-8640

Published by AuthorHouse 09/06/2018

ISBN: 978-1-5462-5696-0 (sc)
ISBN: 978-1-5462-5695-3 (e)

Library of Congress Control Number: 2018909994

Print information available on the last page.

Any people depicted in stock imagery provided by Getty Images are models, and such images are being used for illustrative purposes only. Certain stock imagery © Getty Images.

This book is printed on acid-free paper.

Scripture quotations marked KJV are from the Holy Bible, King James Version (Authorized Version). First published in 1611. Quoted from the KJV Classic Reference Bible, Copyright © 1983 by The Zondervan Corporation.

TABLE OF CONTENTS

"When life hands you those yellow sour things…
get your glass ready to make things a little sweeter!"

– Terran Jordan

Acknowledgments

I am grateful to be able to share my heart with each reader who endeavors to find true success. God is my ultimate source of success. Without him I am truly nothing. A special thanks to my mother, who holds a very special place in my heart. Over the years I have watched and admired her tenacity to keep going, no matter what and persist in her uniqueness. Thank you mom!

To each person who has added value to my life experience knowingly or unknowingly, thank you! I see the good in each lemon peel; some were sweet, while others – well let's just say I had to pucker a little. I have grown to see the fruit of love, joy, peace, longsuffering, gentleness, goodness, faith, meekness, and temperance manifest in my life.

I cannot forget my family immediate or extended. Thank you from the top of my heart for allowing me to be who God created me to be, even if I am just a smidgen of being too serious at times! Thanks for showing me how to have a little fun!

All glory be to God for allowing me to dig deep and experience the success that he has deemed good for me to have! Thank you Father! Amen!

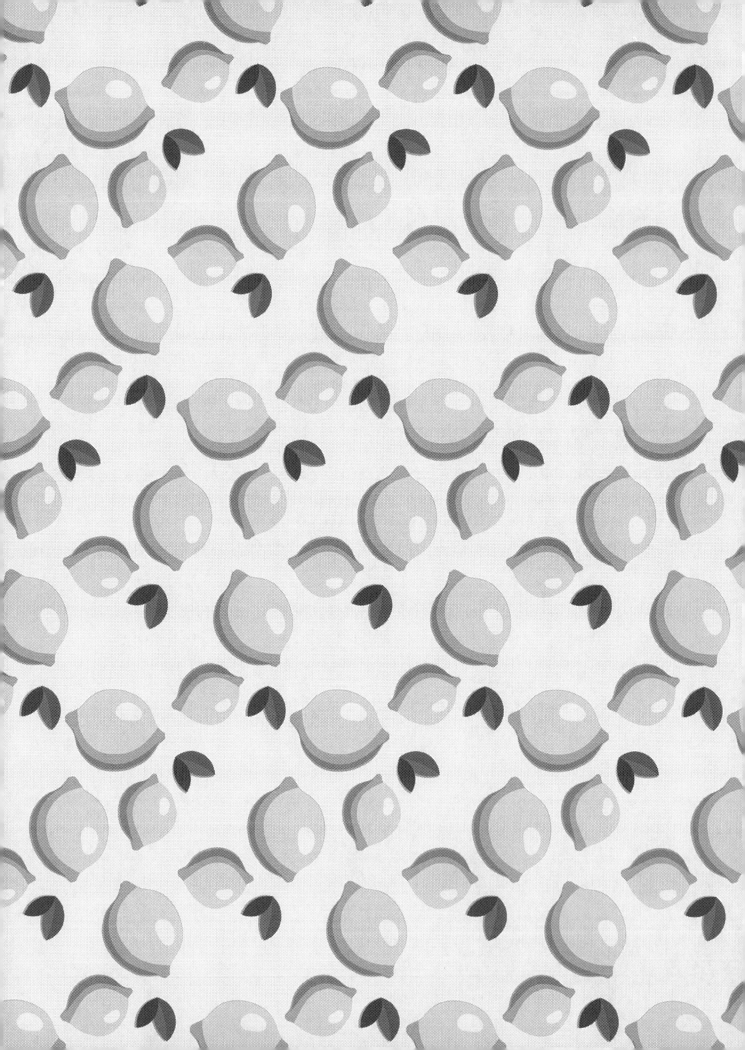

Preface

All too often I found myself "trying" to be successful, but missed the actual opportunity of being successful of where I was. I began the journey of writing this book seven years ago, not knowing that the quest would lead me to finding out that I was already what I was searching for—Success. I labeled myself as an under achiever and knew in my heart that I was not living life at my fullest potential. Then one day during my prayer time with God, after a frustrating week at "trying" to be what I saw everyone else do so effortlessly, God began showing me what he deemed to be success.

God defined success in a way that made a light bulb go off in my brain. I had, for so many years, sought after the world's success and believed it's lie of being inadequate if I did not have a home of my own, drove a top of the line vehicle, and networked my way up the corporate ladder. God essentially showed me who I was through his point of view. I was already successful. That's right. God fashioned me and molded me to be unique on purpose, before I ever went to college or started working in the business and finance arenas. He made me see that the power within my DNA (Destined Noble Achiever) carried more weight than my four year bachelor's degree. That meant that no matter what, I could never fail.

I ask that you take the words written in each page to heart, even as you learn what real success truly means. Remember, adversity can always start out with something bitter, but the steps you follow in the process can make the outcome sweet!

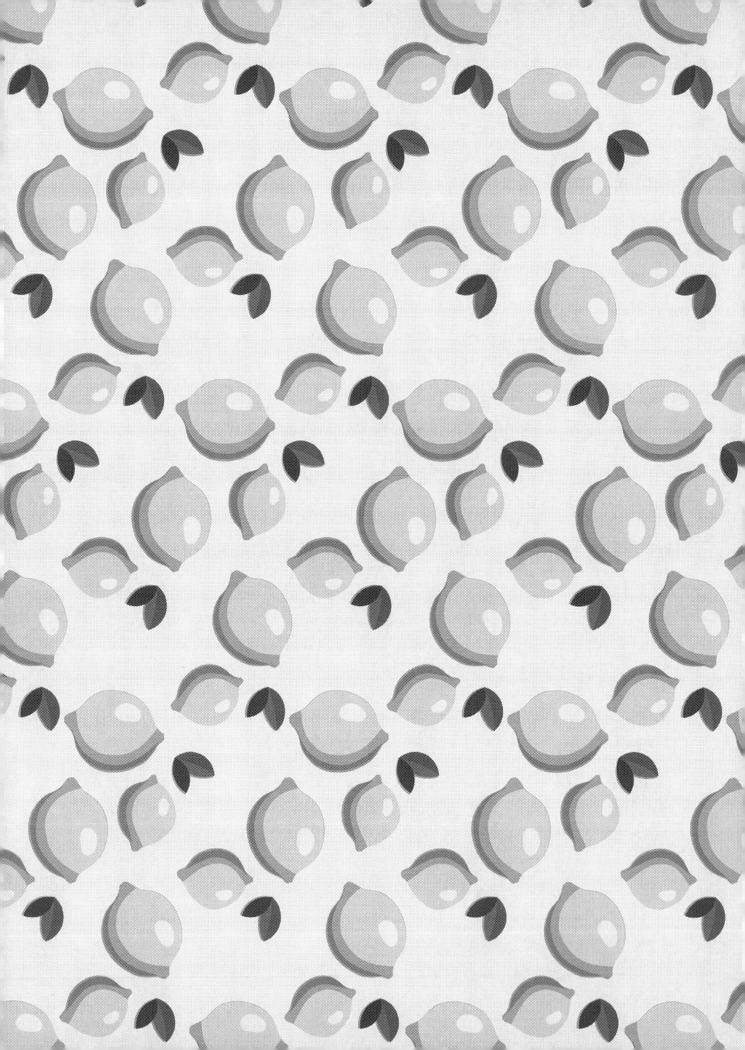

Preface

All too often I found myself "trying" to be successful, but missed the actual opportunity of being successful of where I was. I began the journey of writing this book seven years ago, not knowing that the quest would lead me to finding out that I was already what I was searching for—Success. I labeled myself as an under achiever and knew in my heart that I was not living life at my fullest potential. Then one day during my prayer time with God, after a frustrating week at "trying" to be what I saw everyone else do so effortlessly, God began showing me what he deemed to be success.

God defined success in a way that made a light bulb go off in my brain. I had, for so many years, sought after the world's success and believed it's lie of being inadequate if I did not have a home of my own, drove a top of the line vehicle, and networked my way up the corporate ladder. God essentially showed me who I was through his point of view. I was already successful. That's right. God fashioned me and molded me to be unique on purpose, before I ever went to college or started working in the business and finance arenas. He made me see that the power within my DNA (Destined Noble Achiever) carried more weight than my four year bachelor's degree. That meant that no matter what, I could never fail.

I ask that you take the words written in each page to heart, even as you learn what real success truly means. Remember, adversity can always start out with something bitter, but the steps you follow in the process can make the outcome sweet!

Chapter 1

Prepare For The Inevitable

Sometimes we are not always prepared for the "sour" moments in our lives. Sure, we may have all of the "ingredients" to make life more refreshing, but we never factor in whether there is a defect in our tools or a lack of knowledge in how to use those tools. For example, let's look at the process of making lemonade. Making lemonade should be easy and its ingredients should be accessible to anyone who wishes to make it. The tools and ingredients necessary to make this classic drink are: lemons, sugar, water, pitcher, stirring spoon, juicer/squeezer (optional), and ice (optional). Seems simple right? However, in order for the outcome of this recipe to be successful, you must first be willing to make it. The biggest ingredient of success is having an active desire or want. In other words, you must have the right measurements (goals), the right ingredients, and the zeal to make it happen.

In all things there is a process, but you must have a plan of how you're going to carry out that process. As believers our biggest instructor on how we are to carry out our life's assignment is the Holy Spirit. Yes, that's right! You must first consult God–the originator of your life and its purpose, before making any plan. His strategies will produce the sweetest outcome that you have ever tasted and your first step is called submission. He is the one who knows your ending before your beginning. Now that's amazing!

In the book of Proverbs, Solomon shares with us the benefits of having God's wisdom:

> "5 Trust in the Lord with all thine heart, and lean not unto thine own understanding. 6 In all thy ways acknowledge him, and he shall direct thy paths. 7 Be not wise in thine own eyes: fear the Lord, and depart from evil. 8 It shall be health to thy navel, and marrow to thy bones."
> (Proverbs 3:5-8, KJV)

Within those verses are compelling truths that we should follow in life. When we place our trust in God and not our own selves, acknowledging him along the way, then he can direct us and bring health to our bodies. Such an awesome Father, who would care for his creation! We must stop to ponder on the direction that we consider being right for our lives. Ask yourself, "Did I really hear from God on this matter?" Do we ever ask him about the things that he would like for us to do; even though he created and made the day that we are living in? Do we wait to receive insight from him in our day-to-day functions? Lastly, could we have accomplished more or could the outcome have been better if we followed his voice?

All of these questions create the framework or pattern that should be followed every moment, of every second, of every day. This does not mean that you question or doubt yourself. It simply means that you take your desires, your thoughts and plans to him, submitting them to whatever he says to do with it. That's right; it will bring us to the inevitable–surrendering our will to his will. Jesus himself followed that same due order, with this profound statement made by him in the Garden of Gethsemane, before undertaking the harsh assignment of being crucified: "...not my will, but thine, be done." (Luke 22:42, KJV)

Oftentimes the bitterness or aftermath of life's storms try to overtake, contaminate, sabotage, and distract us from getting up and pressing forward into the things that God has called for us to do. This bitter taste that adversity or tribulation can become a hindrance to our participation of the restoration process we were meant to be partakers in.

**Note: God never made mankind to go through storms, but he intended when storms arise, they go through mankind.

Our adversary, satan, comes in the form of a storm, to intimidate the sons of God. God has given those same sons the authority to rule over him (our adversary). God's recipe for life ends with the result of success, not subjection. Believe it or not, what may seem bitter or hard to swallow, can have a sweet after taste that is enjoyable. From experiences in life, I have learned that there are not always going be sweet tasting days. There will be some sour moments that will cause you to pucker and suck your tongue in disgust.

However to have a clear understanding of how to remove the bitter taste of what has taken place in your life and enjoy the sweet savor of peaceful refreshment:

a. You must first have a renewed mind.

> "2 And be not conformed to this world: but be ye transformed by the renewing of your mind, that ye may prove what is that good, and acceptable, and perfect, will of God." (Romans 12:2, KJV)

b. Secondly, you must be willing.

> "12 For if there be first a willing mind, it is accepted according to that a man hath, and not according to that he hath not." (2 Corinthians 8:12, KJV)

You must use the faith God has equipped you with, in order to see a positive, more rewarding outcome or result. We as Christians find this step so hard to understand at times, when faced with adversity. We know the word, we've heard the word, but do we really believe the word? To begin believing, we must know our God given authority, through faith.

> "17 So then faith cometh by hearing, and hearing by the word of God." (Romans 10: 17, KJV)

In its time, all things have a way of working together. We must not be foolish enough to mix the wrong things together, in order to make our own recipe. You may not get your desired result. Some even get mad at the person who gave a recipe that they tried to follow. It is not the recipe maker that made the error, the finger is now pointed back at our own selves for trying to become a mad scientist and mix our own ingredients together. We must follow the order of steps that God has set before us in its entirety. Imagine making lemonade without lemons. Hard to fathom, right? To remove the main ingredients of any recipe alters the intended purpose.

We can use an illustration of this in the following scenario:

Meet Pam. Pam is an accomplished entrepreneur, philanthropist, thespian, and financial advisor to many well known matriarchs in today's pop culture. As a child Pam grew up with Godly principles and as a college graduate, pursued and succeeded in everything that she put her mind to. She always asked God for direction before taking on any task and flourished because of that. Now Pam is at the peak of her well-established career. She is noted on all prominent websites, telecasts, periodicals, magazines, books, newspapers–you name it.

But as Pam reached the height of her success, she slowly got so entangled with the business of her life, she stopped doing the business of God. Several months into joining in a partnership with her financial planning venture, she found herself still in those same media outlets, but now for being investigated in a money laundering scheme her partner involved their company in. Pam never saw this coming.

As a result, she lost major clients, all of her finances and assets that were tied to her business were frozen, her marriage became strained, her children were being followed from school by the paparazzi, and everything in her life began going in a downward spiral. All she could do was weep from the torment and confusion. This all could have been avoided or prevented, had Pam not left out the key ingredient for her success–GOD.

The scenario used above is not to say that Pam would have never gone through anything, but it does show how she could have gotten keen insight on the financial partnership that she entered into and what was going on with the business. What you have just read is sadly found common amongst most believers. We may start out walking out the steps towards God's will, but lose connection somehow, by the lime light going on around us. God's reality does encompass a light, but that light is his glory that guides us to the places that we are called to be in, with the people we are called to be with.

Even still, if we veer off in the wrong direction, we have an escape method called grace. Grace is what causes us to function and operate with ease and it re-directs us back onto the path that God intended for us to walk on. Paul relays in 2 Corinthians 12:8-9, the strength that God imparts to us all, by his grace. God, in this one instance, satisfies and supplies a measure that keeps his people in equal balance to make living a success.

"8 For this thing I besought the Lord thrice, that it might depart from me. 9 And he said unto me, My grace is sufficient for thee: for my strength is made perfect in weakness. Most gladly therefore will I rather glory in my infirmities, that the power of Christ may rest upon me." (2 Corinthians 12:8-9, KJV)

Chapter 2
The Guide

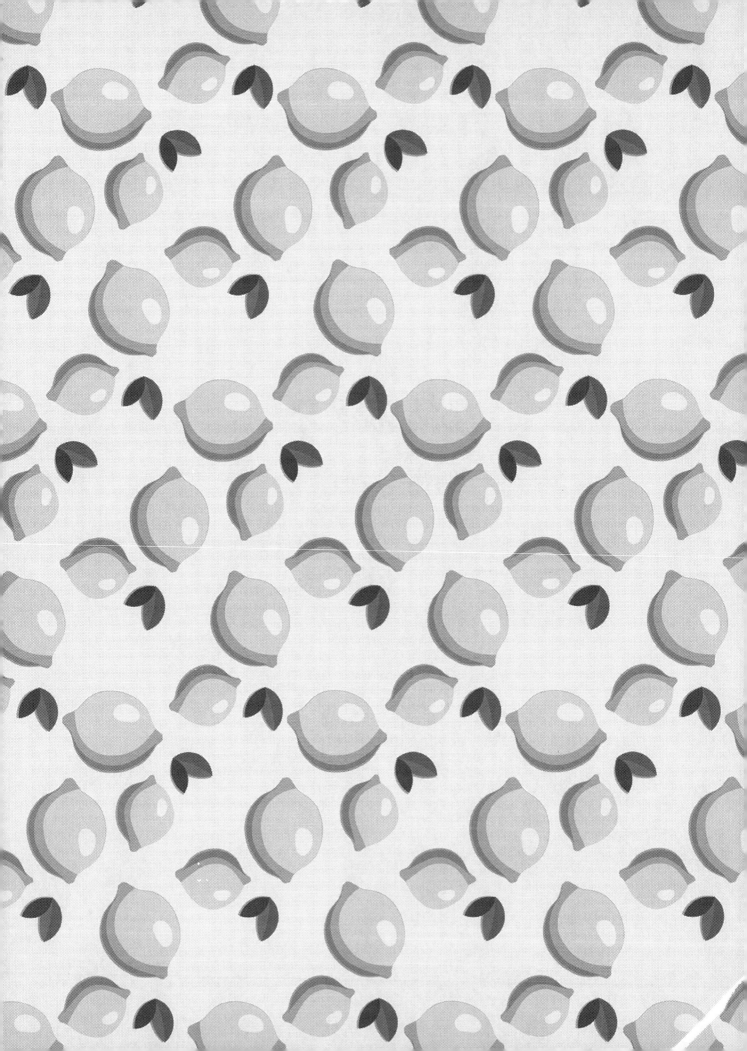

"And thine ears shall hear a word behind thee saying,
This is the way, walk ye in it, when ye turn
to the right hand, and when ye turn to the left."

(Isaiah 30:21, KJV)

The Holy Spirit is part of our kingdom inheritance; this is the main tool for the process. We can then bring the other ingredients together for the sweet expectation. Romans 8:14 assures us that as we walk in unity with the Holy Spirit as our constant companion, we will remain connected as sons and daughters of God.

We are also reminded in verse 28 of Chapter 8 that all things will work together when we keep our love and affection towards God. Bearing the fruit of patience during the process is needful when carrying out God's due order of fulfillment. I believe that patience was designed to capture the gracefulness of wisdom. What we do in patience seems so insignificant, but the wait holds so much power and strength.

"In your patience possess ye your souls." (Luke 21:19, KJV)

Don't allow the bitterness of life's experiences to change how you view your self-worth. Why would I write such a statement? The word of God requires us to use faith to believe that what God has spoken, will actually manifest. Along with faith, confidence or hope is necessary in the completion of God's will–his word.

"35 Cast not away therefore your confidence, which hath great recompense of reward. 36 For ye have need of patience, that, after ye have done the will of God ye might receive the promise." (Hebrews 10:35-36, KJV)

The prophet Isaiah enlightens us with this evidence, in his plight to those who seek desperately for the presence of God:

> "So shall my word be that goeth forth out of my mouth: it shall not return unto me void, but it shall accomplish that which I please, and it shall prosper in the thing whereto I sent it."

(Isaiah 55:11, KJV)

Here is another illustration:

Imagine that you go to a farm and notice the farmer's wife dressing a pig in ladies trousers, a bonnet, and high-heeled shoes. She then proceeds to pierce the pig's ears, placing 24 kt diamond earrings in them. As you watch in bewilderment, the farmer's wife continues in this absurd behavior, by arching the pig's eyebrows, penciling in and defining them with eyeliner, and adding dashes of eye shadow, rouge and lipstick!! By this time the pig has had enough and begins to run-a-muck, splashing and waddling in a nearby mud hole!

I hope you get the picture now. All of the woman's effort and time did not negate the fact that God made the pig to be a pig–not a human! Now, if God has taken the time to distinguish the attributes of an animal from the attributes of a human being, what makes us think that his making us into his image would negate that we have his very same character?

> "26 And God said, Let us make man in our image, after our likeness: and let them have dominion over the fish of the sea, and over the fowl of the air, and over the cattle, and over all the earth, and over every creeping thing that creepeth upon the earth. 27 So God created man in his own image, in the image of God created he him; male and female created he them."

> (Genesis 1: 26-27, KJV)

Our trials and tribulations will never change how God made or intended for us to be. We are worth more than our current circumstance. God breathed his very essence and life source on the inside of us! We are the apple of his eye! When we stop trying to prove who we are and surrender ourselves to God, we will have sweet encounters of success!

We must get rid of the excessive need to get approval to be who we are, from mankind. Our approval has already been given by God. At times we are so bound by the opinion of others; we allow their will to take the place of God's. In a sense, they become our Holy Spirit, directing our lives and thinking. Consulting anyone without presenting the matter before our heavenly Father produces an autonomous way of thinking. For as a man thinks, that's what he becomes (Proverbs 23:7).

Since 2008, I had been trying to reach for success through networking, gaining my Life Insurance License and promoting my knowledge, skills, and abilities to many local businesses in the DC/MVA area. To my disappointment, all I could foster were a bunch of low-end sales jobs. I became even the more eager and persistent working for a temp agency. The success hunt was relentless and never-ending. I remember staying up long hours during the night, surfing the web and even praying to God that he would intervene.

It wasn't until the early months of 2011, that I began to realize that I never asked God what he wanted me to do and what his assignment for me was. I spent almost three years telling God what he should do for me, not knowing I was in disobedience by not listening to the direction of the Holy Spirit. That's another thing that I learned, that you can override the promptings of the Holy Spirit.

When we allow God's agenda to embrace us and cast away our own, we will start to see the full manifestations that God intended for us to experience.

Here is a prayer that God led me to pray, which kept my focus on his plan:

"Father, I come to you humble and broken. Forgive me for not allowing you to lead my life. I present myself back to you. Take my life and transform every part to be in accordance with your will. I submit totally to you and you alone. I accept your refreshing words to revive me once again, that I may walk your perfect way. Here I am Lord, use me. In your name I pray, Amen."

Chapter 3

The Power

Are you using the power that God has given you, in order to use your spiritual tools effectively? Whether you realize it or not, you have power. That same power was imprinted on the inside of you from the beginning of time (Genesis 1:26-28, KJV):

> 26 And God said, Let us make in our image, after our likeness: and let them have dominion... So God created man in his own image, in the image of God created he him; male and female created he them. 28 And God blessed them and God said unto them, 'Be fruitful, and multiply, and replenish the earth, and subdue it; and have dominion.

Now let's look at some very key words here:

"And God said" = the word 'and' is used to join one finite verb to another, so that together they are equivalent to an infinitive of purpose. The word 'God' is defined as a supreme reality. The word 'said' is past tense of the word say, which means to pronounce or is a power of decision. "subdue it" = the word 'subdue' means to bring under control. The word 'it' is whatever is a plant, person, animal, or abstract entity. "have dominion" = The word 'have' means to hold at a disadvantageous position or one that has material wealth. The word 'dominion' simply means to rule or have supreme authority.

So to sum it all up, God gave humanity an opportunity of a lifetime (literally), that would place us right smack dab in the middle of success. All we need to do is grab a hold of it with the power of our faith and begin to walk it out. The words within themselves have so much power, just think if we were to believe in the words that were spoken over us and let them be the force of our daily conversations! Some other important words that have a powerful meaning are exusia and dunamus.

Exusia means to exercise authority and dunamus is God's irrefutable power. With these two words joined together, it further explains God's original intent for man:

The supreme reality gave a power of decision to extend to man, the right to bring under control: every lifeless thing, plant, animal, or abstract thing. To hold in a disadvantageous position, having material wealth and supreme authority, to exercise God's irrefutable power.

I encourage you to read that statement of truth again, and again, and again, until it marinates within your soul. In order for you to use that type of authority, however, you must first know who you are. If you are in a position of authority, but know who you are, the authority given to you is useless. Almost as useless as giving you a license to drive a car, yet you insist on walking, even though you have the keys, the vehicle, and the authority to do so.

We have been given a license by God to occupy the earth with power and authority. The problem with that liberty is that some of us are only occupying the earth and not ruling in the earth. God has equipped us all to so many extraordinary things within the earth realm, but we must first get back to the basics of our understanding of why we exist.

Sour moments in life will come and they will go, but we must not get intimidated by their presence. They are abstract entities that are subject to us and we have the power to change them into something sweet.

I'm reminded of a time within my own personal life. I had just moved to the state of Maryland from North Carolina in 2008. I came up-state hoping and expecting a change in my life that would alter the past few months of turmoil and distress. I was still getting over a failed relationship, with a person I was engaged to be married. My own agenda soon came to a screeching halt, after a year of unsuccessfully locating a career in finance. I even tried getting reinstated within the federal government. Soon things got even worse, and all I could find were very-low end sales jobs that barely paid my rent or car payments. My health began to decline and the stress of it all brought me to a place of depression. I felt power-less.

This all happened in just a few months, but there was a silver lining to all of this mayhem. I found an awesome church and began studying the word of God like never before. Yet still, I held on to the hope of one day reaching that long-sought-for success I thought would make me invincible.

It wasn't until 2 1/2 years later that the veil, which clung so very tightly over my eyes, was removed. After all this time a sense of understanding and wisdom flooded my mind. I was looking for success by natural means and understanding. In order to walk in God's arena of success, I had to use spiritual wisdom and kingdom authority. I realized that I was allowing life to invade me on earth's terms and not heaven's.

Real success is when you begin to walk and live from heaven to earth and not earth to heaven. I began to accept that my citizenship in heaven was just as active and valid as my citizenship was here in the United States. I had to start tapping into my God given Power of Authority (P.O.A.) here on earth. Naturally, a person who has Power of Attorney oversees, with discretion, the affairs of a person who is still living; but has granted authority to another person or party to handle his or her business transactions or decisions.

As stewards of God in Christ, we have been given the same power and authority as ambassadors here on the earth, to represent God's kingdom in heaven.

4 But God, who is rich in mercy, for his great love wherewith he loved us, 5 Even when we were dead in sins, hath quickened us together with Christ (by grace are ye saved) 6 And has raised us up together, and made us sit together in heavenly places in Christ Jesus.

Ephesians 2:4-6, KJV God, who with his infinitive sovereignty, has chosen man to partake in his kingship. God's authoritative command still rules earth's atmosphere eons after, "And God said, 'Let there be'.....

Now let's operate in that kingship, by activating that power. Don't be intimidated any longer. Turn on the switch. Say this out loud (no matter where you are; they'll think you're singing anyway):

"I'VE GOT THE POWER!!!!" Go ahead, you can smile. The joy of the Lord is your strength (power)!

Chapter 4

What's In Your Hand?

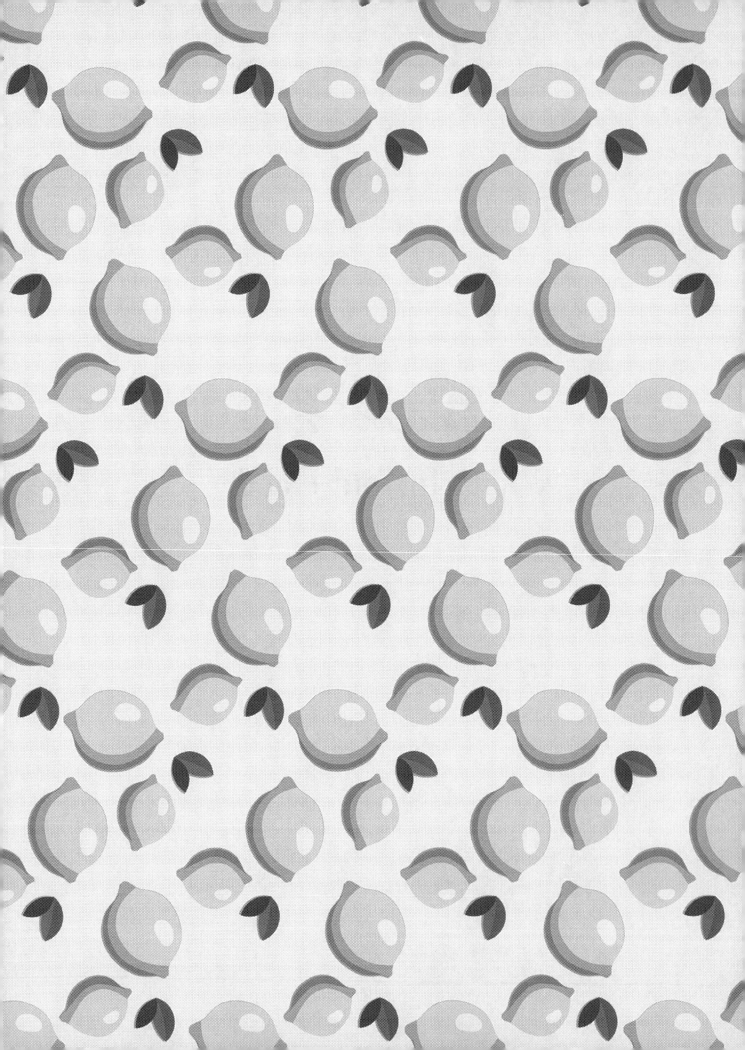

Many times we look to others for a helping hand. Truth be told, we all need assistance from each other at some point in our lives. Our parents are one source; friends or other family members could be another. Just what am I getting at, you say? Our dependence on others can create a long-term crutch, if we aren't mindful of what we consider as a helping hand or our go-to when things seem to be going downhill. Our constant, full, complete, and total dependence should always be on God–period.

Total security in the one who created you, with the end in mind, is the only remedy for your life's success; without substitutes (Isaiah 46:10). God has given everything you need right at your fingertips. I know, I know. You're probably looking at your hands and saying, "At my fingertips, aye? All I can see are calluses from working so darn hard and that I'm badly in need of a manicure!" Well maybe you're not saying exactly that, but you get my point right? Hands are essential for anyone who works. Besides, "the kingdom of God is at hand"! Your hands to be exact!

> 19 And I will give unto thee the keys of the kingdom of heaven: and whatsoever thou shalt bind on earth shall be bound in heaven: and whatsoever thou shalt loose on earth shall be loosed in heaven.

> Matthew 16:19, KJV

Do you know how successful you really are? I pray the insight from this book will open your mind to the truth of this knowledge. Journey with me to the story of Moses, when God commanded that he should lead the people of Israel into the Promised Land. He asked a very distinct question to Moses and that was, "What is that in thine hand?" We see, from the beginning in Genesis Chapter 3, that when God poses a question to man, it's not that he doesn't already know the answer. We must put away our own reasoning in order to grasp what is really happening in both of those contexts. Each instance initiated a series of God's revealing power, in order to get the spiritual attention of the individual he was questioning. Taking a closer look at Chapter 4 of Exodus, God used several illustrations by signs, wonders, and miracles, using the hands of Moses. Moses felt incapable of doing what God was telling him he could do. Ultimately, the power that God has so freely given to us is his alone.

God also wants us to be partakers of his infinite power to show us his love purposed for our lives. "For in him we live, move, and have our being" (Acts 17:28). God wants us to know that he designed us to house his power, though we must come to a renewed mind in order to understand and contain it. It is difficult for someone to exact power if they don't know how to use or appropriate it. The keys have been given to us, so now we must learn how to use them.

The first step is reading the instruction manual–the Bible (2Timothy 2:15).

Secondly, we must meditate on the word of God (Joshua 1:8). Thirdly, we must speak the words that we have studied and meditated on; not parokeeting it, but speaking boldly in faith (Romans 10:8; Matthew 4:4; Psalm 19:14). Lastly, we must become the word of God (2Corinthians 3:2).

When you become what God has said you are, you embrace all of who he is in the kingdom of God. So many people look at the process of obtaining power from a worldly perspective. They strive towards becoming a high ranking official, marking their prestige with awards, ribbons, and trophies.

True power is only effective when the possessor humbly acknowledges it's source, being not of their own selves, but of the one who gave it to them. Some obtain power by walking on the backs of others and not allowing them to stand on their shoulders. So what's the difference? The difference is that the one, who stands on the shoulders of others, has someone holding them up, keeping them balanced. If the person underneath them would move from their position, the person standing on their shoulders would fall. It's called accountability and with accountability you have a support system. One with the right intensions and in turn will move you to do the same for someone else.

The person who walks on the backs of others will never reach the height of success they so arrogantly strive for. The will never be able to get a chance to view the top from a difference perspective. It is God who gives us life, power, and wealth. Although we have at our fingertips, these things, it is necessary not to forget that very thing (Deuteronomy 8:17-18). We must not assume that we are God's gift to the world, when in fact; we share in the gift of Christ; who was given to the world to redeem mankind back to his intended state.

The state of authority usurped before the fall of man in the Garden of Eden. Just imagine that at the very hand of God man was formed and at the hand of man, all of creation groans for the supernatural manifestations of power. Creation groans because we have not fully grasped the concept of who we are and who we were created to be. We have purpose and an inheritance to help us fulfill that very purpose. Statement of Purpose:

I have God's uniquely designed purpose operating in my life. I stand in faith in receiving all that I need to fulfill his divine purpose in my life. Distractions will not deter me from my orchestrated destiny. I am in perfect alignment with the words God has spoken concerning me. I strive not for accolades obtained by prideful coercions. I am true to who God intended for me to be. I acknowledge that I am an heir to throne of God by Christ Jesus. I will always give thanks and glory to God, for it is HIS will that shall be manifested in the earth through me.

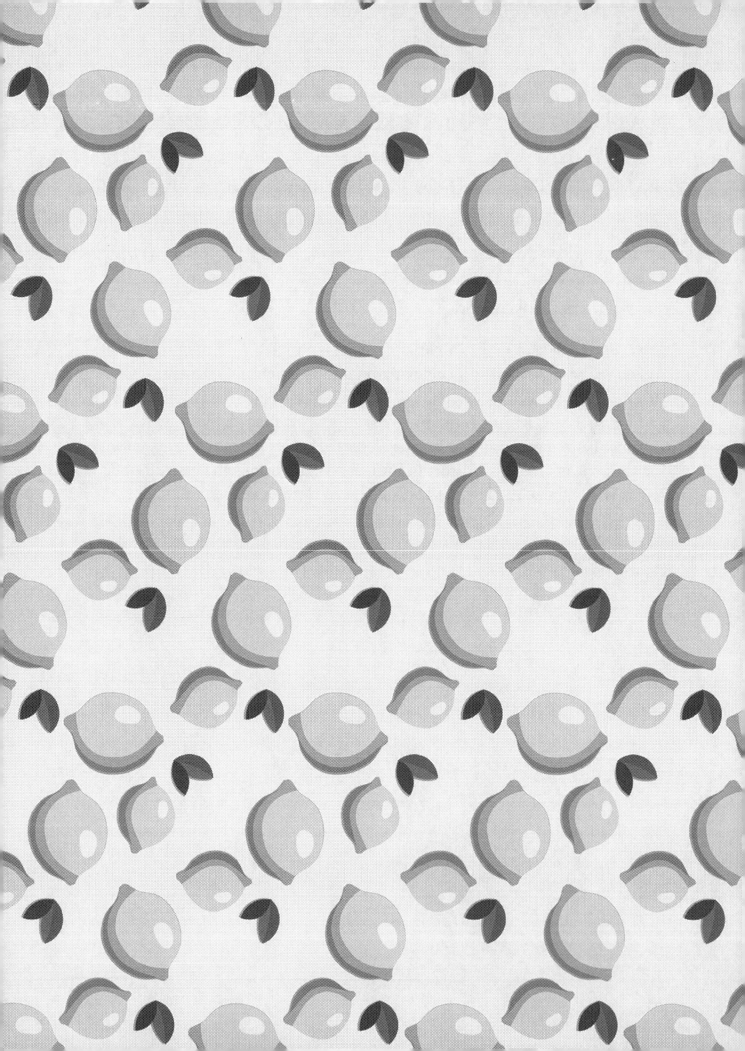

Chapter 5
No Substitutes

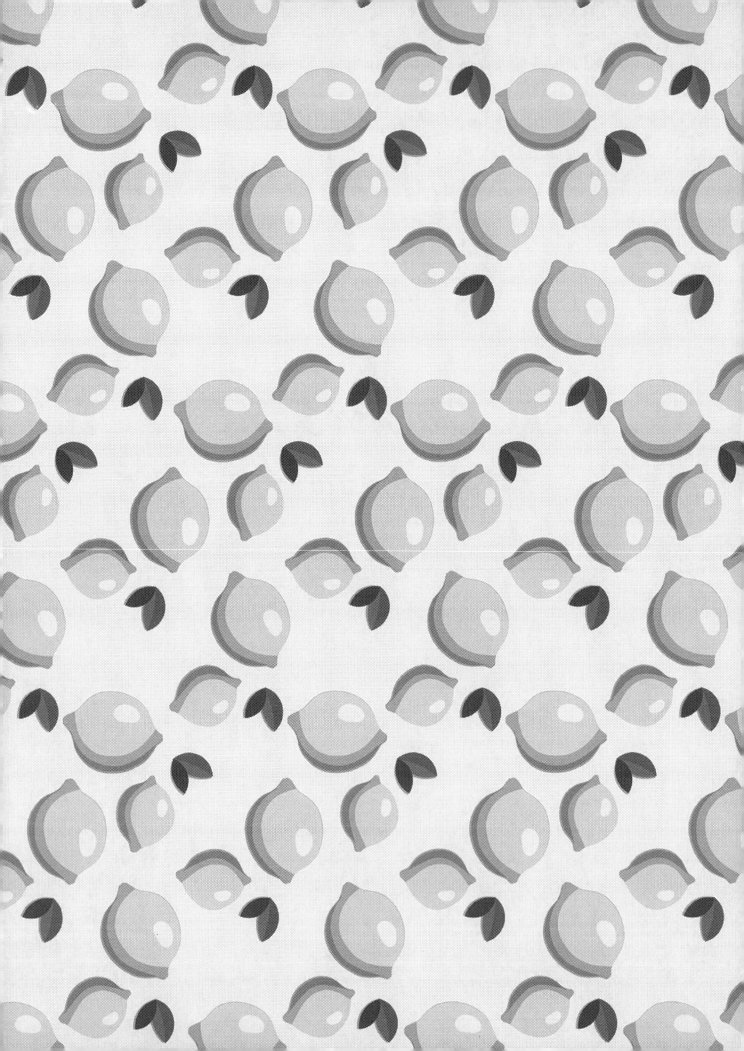

Generally speaking, all recipes have a specific format or formula to follow. If any ingredient is missing, you will not end up with the same result that the recipe is calling for. There are times when the recipe allows substitutes to replace a certain ingredient. This is of course an alternative to the original. The creator of the recipe tested and experimented with the suggested substitute, before recommending its inclusion during the preparation.

Just like those substitutes for those recipes, the law in the Old Testament allowed for substitutes to take the place of what was originally intended. It allow bulls and goats to stand proxy for the sins of man. Year after year, the priest would continually perform rituals to cover the sins of man with these animals as substitutes. These substitutes were only a temporary fix and God that no substitute would ever satisfy the debt of sin that man committed. Mankind needed the real thing—a savior.

He invites you to partake of the sweetest refreshment you've ever tasted. Growing up "down south" we went to a corner store, which was only about a ten minute walk from where we lived.

The store was actually inside one of our neighbor's homes and we would only go when our Nana wasn't making her infamous flavored ice cups. Of course our neighbor didn't mind receiving our business and would gladly take our spare change, but nothing; absolutely nothing was like Nana's homemade sweet concoction!

You could tell that there was love mixed in each slurp of her ice cups that seemed to explode in our mouths! My mother and aunts have since taken on the tradition of Nana's invention food qualities. God's love is evident too, through the death, burial, and resurrection of Jesus Christ.

A Refreshing Thought:

Embrace the truth of God's love and add him to the recipe of your life today. You won't regret the end results.

> 5 Trust in the Lord with all thine heart; and lean not unto thine own understanding. 6 In all thy ways acknowledge him, and he shall direct thy paths. 7 Be not wise in thine own eyes: fear the LORD, and depart from evil. 8 It shall be health to thy navel, and marrow to thy bones.
>
> Proverbs 3:5-8, KJV

Chapter 6
Measured 2 Capacity

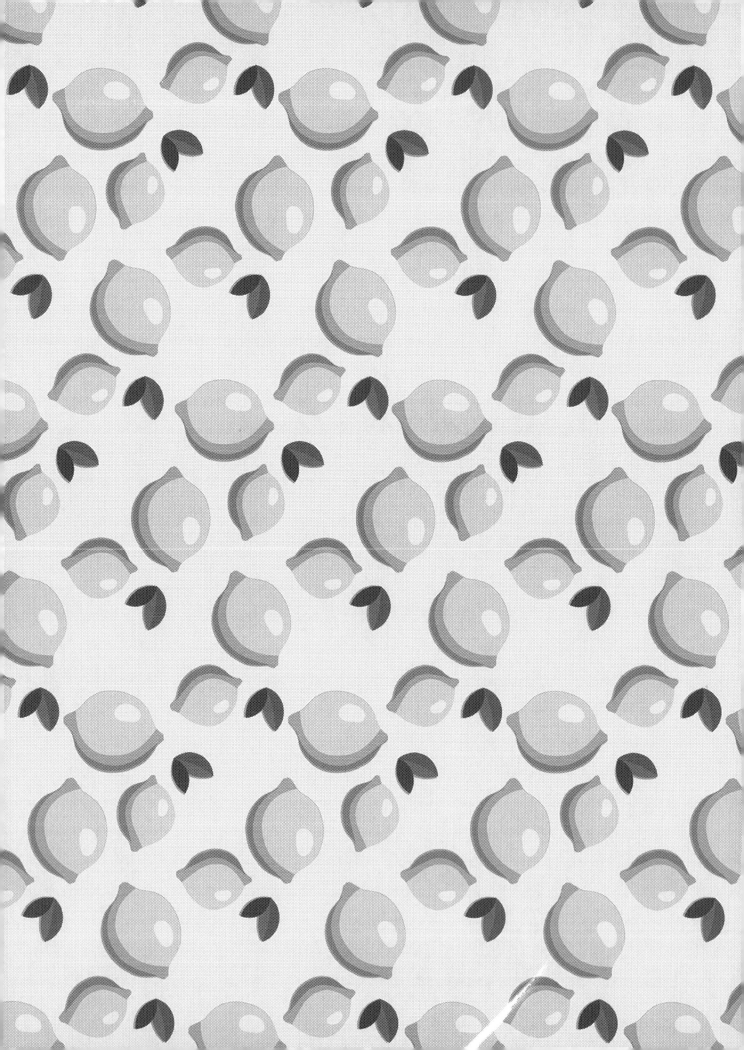

Waiter: "What type of drink are you having today ma'am?" **Christina:** "Ahhh, let's see. Which drinks do you have free refills on?"

Waiter: "Well all of our fountain drinks have as many refills as you want."

Christina: "Great! I'll try them all then!"

Waiter: "Sure, give me a few seconds and I'll get that right out to you!"

Imagine for a moment that the waiter is Jesus and you are Christina:

Emmanuel: "Welcome to Chez Heavenly. My name is Emmanuel. May I get you some of our finest thirst quenching beverage?"

Christina: "Wow, you sure sound confident! Are any refills on this amazing drink?"

Emmanuel: "No."

Christina: "What?"

Emmanuel: "No, there aren't any refills."

Christina: "Excuse me. Did you just say that this amazing drink has no refills?"

Emmanuel: "Yes. If it were not so, I would have told you." **Christina:** "And I bet it costs an arm and a leg. How much is it?" **Emmanuel:** "Actually it costs more than an arm and a leg, but here at Chez Heavenly, it's offered free to anyone who desires to have it."

Christina: "Wait a minute. You mean to tell me this unbelievably, thirst quenching, amazing drink is free to everyone? It must be nasty!"

Emmanuel: "No beloved, it's actually the quite opposite. For when you drink this particular beverage, you'll never thirst again. Why don't you taste and see for yourself that it is good?" **Christina:** "Well....what is your name again?"

Emmanuel: "Emmanuel, but you can call me Manny for short." **Christina:** "Well, Manny let me try some this never-thirst-again' drink."

Emmanuel: "Coming right up, according to your words!"

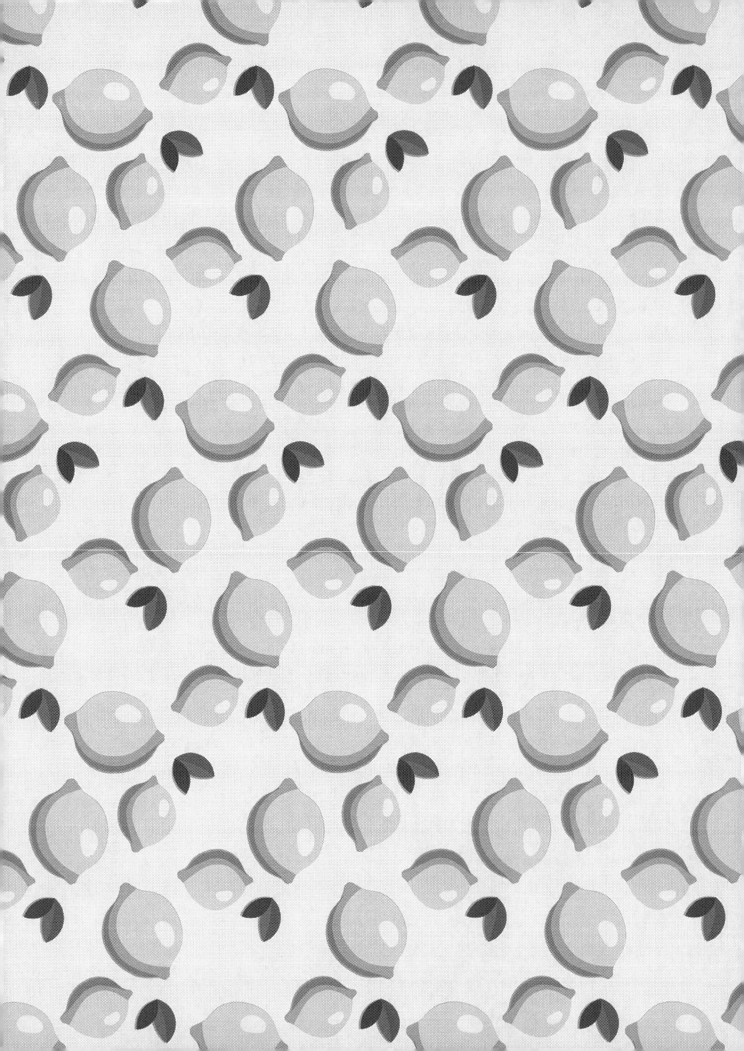

Many Christians still have a hard time understanding the interpretation that Jesus wants to convey in the parable about the Samaritan woman at Jacob's well (John 4:10, KJV). The living water that Jesus was referring to was the Holy Spirit. Some may reason, how that could be, since he had not ascended to heaven and yet still had not even been crucified either. My answer is simply this-BELIEVE!! [Luke 8:50; John 6:35, 37, 44, 47]

The kingdom of God and the promises that he has made are only accessed through faith. Faith is the spiritual vehicle that enables us to receive supernatural things and allows us to manifest it here in the natural. If you're still not convinced, read about the faith of Abraham in Romans Chapter 4, verse 3 and also how we are to please God with our faith Romans Chapter 8, verses 5-8.

The Holy Spirit is our guide, just like a measuring cup. The lines represented on a measuring cup are in essence boundaries that show the user where to stop with the desired portion being poured. The Holy Spirit also directs and guides us of where or how far we should go during our Christian journey. One season of our life may require more measurements or steps than another.

The Lord's Prayer also gives us insight that God wants to provide us with sufficient substance daily. There are new mercies given for each day. These all indicate God's desire to ensure we follow through with the right recipe so that we can succeed and have an abundant life.

God wants each of us to experience the fulfilling love that he has towards us, but first we must open our hearts and believe that he wants to serve us and provide us with good things. He's not angry or mad at any of us. He longs to see us complete and full of joy. He has no pleasure in watching us drink from the sin offering that Satan has portrayed to be satisfying.

He wants to refresh and renew minds and hearts to thirst after the pure and living water that washes clean the tainted taste of sin. Step out in faith and believe that there is a God who is totally head over heels in love with you and is offering an unlimited supply of thirst quenching water.

Repeat this prayer of faith to confirm your new commitment to allow God to be your server and guide:

"Father God, thank you for giving your son Jesus Christ as a servant for me. Help me to receive your grace to be filled with your goodness and to be led by your Holy Spirit. Let me also accept this as a free gift from you to enjoy without feeling undeserving. I pray that I live a life of faith that enables me to access what you have just for me.

In your name I pray, Amen."

Chapter 7

Taste Test

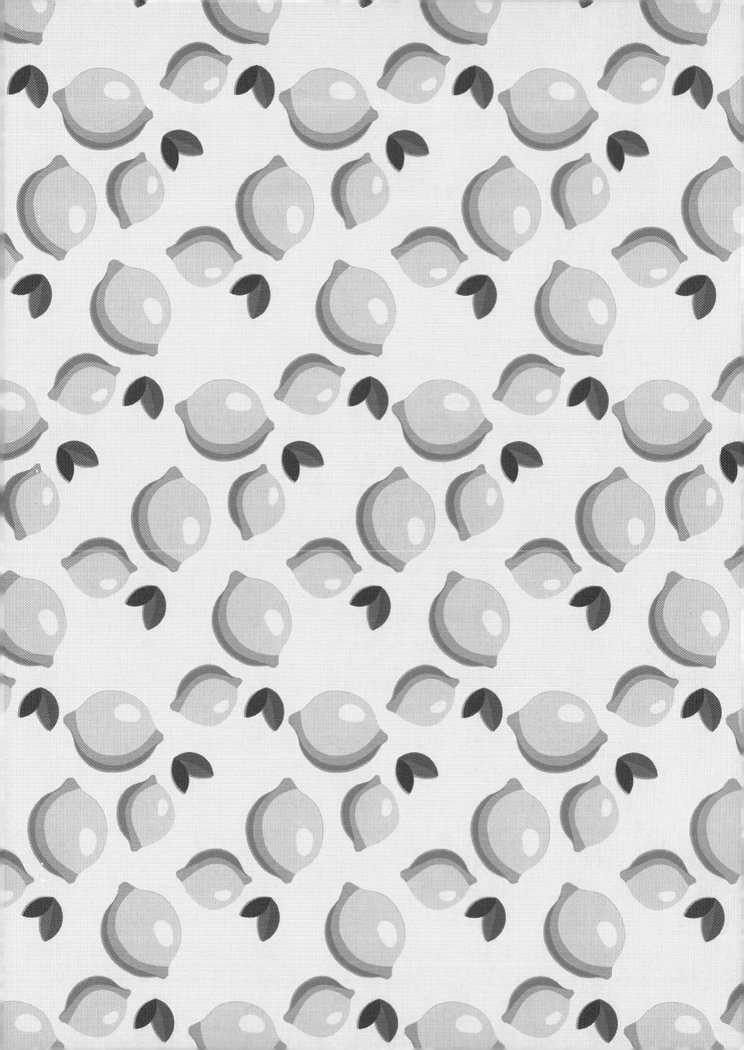

In Chapter 6, we took a look at Jesus being our server. Let's go on another imaginary ride:

You are given a taste testing voucher of a world renowned drink, from a reputable company. A close friend referred you as being one of the primary recipients. The invite seems tempting and sparks your curiosity, so you decide to cash it in. Alas, at the very moment the drink is placed in your hands your tongue licks your lips and you prepare to have your taste buds lavished. As you pucker, your phone rings. Disappointed, you place the drink on the counter and see that you've had several missed calls. You listen to the voicemails and to your surprise your boss needs you to hurry back to the office for an emergency board meeting. Scurrying, you gather your things, cutting your lunch break short and leaving an opportunity of a lifetime in an ice filled glass on the counter top.

Now back from our little imaginary trip. What you've just experienced is an illustration of how many of us spend our lives. Each day, we are presented with choices. Those choices determine how well we live and function, whether good or bad, bountifully or in lack. Take a step back for a moment and ask yourself if the scenario above is currently how your life seems to be. If given the opportunity, would you have at least a sip of the world renowned drink? Or perhaps you would have shrugged it off as a missed opportunity? Maybe you settle in your heart that it wouldn't be worth all of the hype you had been hearing that it was.

The point that I want to make is that sometimes in life we get so frazzled or busy with the day-to-day demands in life, be it our homes, families, or careers that we miss the small moments that could have major impacts on our quality of life. Life is not about reaching the highest pinnacle of modern day achievements, but about how you spend the moments that you think are insignificant. Wouldn't you say that you were shown favor to be one of the primary recipients of that drink? To pass up an opportunity that, in this instance, would then be watered down and no longer tasteful would be a waste.

On average there are between 3,000 to 10,000 taste buds on the human tongue. It's impossible to believe that God would have given us that many if he didn't want us to experience life at different heights and different levels. God is a creative being and foods are a part of his wondrous creation, including drinks. We bypass what God intended to be joyful living by our own preconceived concepts and ideas of how life should be lived. To short change even a nice cool drink of a life time is a way to say to God, I don't want to experience the more that you have for me- it's just a drink.

Every experience of our lives is unique to how God wants us to see his goodness, whether it's being handpicked or selected for a renowned taste testing, or given a first class seat for an airline mix up. We must know that the best part of being a serving is getting the chance to see the person that you are serving is enjoying what you've given them. You want them to partake in the memories that they will have of such an awesome experience and hope that they will return and ask for more.

Don't allow your life to become mundane or routine. Drink from the glass of cool and favorable opportunities that will create a lasting memory in your life. YOU have the power to choose whether success will be sweet or whether it will be sour! The next time you're given a chance of a lifetime, choose the sweet glass of success! I guarantee you will find some refreshment and your life will be a whole lot sweeter!

"Success is not defined as to whether you have material gain or possessions. Real success is having the intestinal fortitude to launch out in faith to achieve what you believe in your heart will make a difference in your life and the lives of others-come hell or high water. It's about setting a legacy that will change not only the course of time, but how life is generally perceived."

– Terran R. M. Jordan

Lemonade Recipes

Raspberry Lemonade

Ingredients:

Serves 8
1 bag of frozen raspberries
11 cups of water
3 ½ cups of sugar

5 cups of freshly squeezed lemon juice
1 Sprig of Mint
Cubed Ice

Step1: Pour 3 cups of water and 3 ½ cups of sugar into a glass pitcher, stirring well. Add 8 more cups of water, along with 5 cups of freshly squeezed lemon juice, ½ sprig of mint and bag of frozen raspberries into mixture. Stir and then place into refrigerator to chill.

Step2: Serve with cubed ice. Garnish with other half of Mint Sprig.

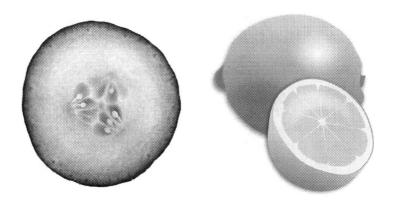

Cucumber Lemonade

Ingredients:

Serves 1
1 Cucumber thinly sliced (10 slices)
1 cup of spring water
½ Orange freshly squeezed
½ of Lime freshly squeezed

1 lemon freshly squeezed
3 tbsp organic honey
1 Rosemary Sprig to garnish
Cubed Ice

Step1: Combine and stir 1 cup of spring water, ½ freshly squeezed orange, ½ freshly squeezed lime, 1 freshly squeezed lemon, 3 tbsp of organic honey and cucumber slices into a tall glass.

Step2: Serve with cubed ice. Garnish with Rosemary Sprig.

Lavender Lemonade

Ingredients:

Serves 4

¼ freshly crushed
Lavender Blossoms

1 ¼ cups of Sugar

1 cup of freshly squeezed lemon juice

4 Lavender Sprigs to garnish

5 cups of water

Cubed Ice

Step1: Bring 2 ½ cups of water to a boil, in a medium saucepan. Remove from heat and add ¼ freshly crushed Lavender Blossoms. Cover and let sit for 20 minutes. Strain Lavender Blossoms from water and discard blossoms.

Step2: Add 1 cup of freshly squeezed lemon juice, lavender blossom water, remaining 2 ½ cups of water, and 1 ¼ cups of sugar into a medium glass pitcher. Stir well and refrigerate for 2 hours.

Step3: Serve in a tall glass with cubed ice. Garnish with Lavender Sprigs.

Strawberry Lemonade

Ingredients:

Serves 10-12
10-12 Strawberries
10 Tarragon Sprigs
2 ¼ cups of Sugar
6 ½ cups of freshly squeezed lemon juice

1 lemon thinly sliced into 14 slices to garnish
11 cups of water
Cubed or Crushed Ice

Step1: Bring 5 cups of water to a boil, in a medium saucepan. Remove from heat and add 6 Tarragon Sprigs. Stir and then let cool for 30 minutes. Remove Tarragon Sprigs.

Step2: Combine 6 cups of remaining water, 6 ½ cups of freshly squeezed lemon juice, 2 ¼ cups of Sugar, and the room temperature Tarragon Sprigs water from saucepan into a large glass pitcher. Mix until sugar is well stirred.

Step3: Slice 6 strawberries in half and stir into mixture. Add the 4 unheated Tarragon Sprigs, 14 lemon slices, and remaining whole strawberries to mixture. Stir.

Step4: Serve in a tall glass with cubed or crushed Ice. Fruit garnish optional.